Erika Knight

KEEP
CALM
AND
CAST
ON

GOOD ADVICE
FOR KNITTERS

Quadrille
PUBLISHING

" Properly practiced, knitting soothes the troubled spirit, and it doesn't hurt the untroubled spirit, either. "

ELIZABETH ZIMMERMANN
WRITER AND KNITTER (1910–1999),
KNITTING WITHOUT TEARS, 1971

While the ball band will give the manufacturer's recommended stitch and row count over a certain measurement, you must also always check your own tension over the stitch pattern to be used. If your tension varies by even one stitch or row from that given in the pattern, change your needle size up or down accordingly. Over a larger piece, any differences will be exaggerated.

Betsan Corkhill, a former physiotherapist, identified that maximum doses of medication for depression were relatively ineffective if issues of low-self esteem and anxiety were not addressed. Going on to work on craft magazines, Betsan was surprised by the volume of readers' correspondence extolling the health benefits of knitting – from reducing pain levels to alleviating suicidal thoughts. Inspired by this anecdotal evidence, Betsan founded Stitchlinks in 2005, an organisation dedicated to researching the therapeutic effects of knitting and stitching.

"Knitting is a distinct virtue. It's reflective and repetitive. Whenever you are engaged in doing a purely repetitive thing, your mind can reflect upon life."

GEOFFREY FISHER (1887–1972)
ARCHBISHOP OF CANTERBURY

If you find the last stitch of your cast-off edge is loose, pointy and looks unsightly, this technique will ensure a neat finish. Cast off the stitches on your final row until just one last stitch remains on the left-hand needle. Place the tip of the right-hand needle into the row below the last stitch on the left-hand needle. Knit this stitch then pull the strand of yarn to tighten the loop. Fasten off the last stitch as usual.

Knit for someone else, such as a charity or a relief effort, and you will enjoy the feel-good factor gained from knowing you have helped someone else. 'Helper's high' is the term coined by Robert Cialdini, Professor of Psychology and Marketing at Arizona State University, to describe the euphoria reported by frequent givers in his research.

"*Knitting… It's like having a nice cup of tea with a big spoonful of honey, isn't it? My childhood was spent rugged up in woolly jumpers and handmade socks, building treehouses, picking blackberries and scooping tadpoles from ponds. When I wasn't building, picking or scooping, I was tucked up next to the fire, watching my Mum and my Nanna making those very socks and jumpers. Their needles clacked and they chattered, we sipped tea and stared at the fire. It felt cosy and safe and happy and right. Knitting is a link back to those clacky, cosy days. Knitting is about the happy colourful nostalgia and my own personal history. It's a comfort, a meditation and a nod to the ladies I love the most.* **"**

PIP LINCOLNE

PROPRIETOR OF MEET ME AT MIKES,
WRITER, BLOGGER AND KNITTER

A good friend always says "Every fault a fashion." By this she means, do not regard your 'mistakes' as errors, instead turn them into creative learning experiences. This lesson has stood me in very good stead over my years and experiments as a knitter.

Stitchlinks aims to help everyone to live a positive life, not only those with a diagnosed medical condition. Using their chosen tools of knitting, stitching and crochet, the practise of a craft can benefit even those who are fit and healthy, enhancing their wellbeing and encouraging positive living.

"*Then she picked up her knitting and began to knit, slowly at first, since her fingers were stiff and rheumatic when she first awoke, but very soon her pace grew faster, and her fingers lost their painful stiffness. 'Another day,' said Miss Marple to herself, greeting the fact with her usual gentle pleasure.***"**

AGATHA CHRISTIE
WRITER (1890–1976),
AT BETRAM'S HOTEL, 1965

The rhythmic repetitive action of knitting is beneficial in tangibly managing stress, pain and depression, and even strengthening the body's immune system.

There are many different methods for sewing up a garment: choose the one that best suits your particular project, based on the content of the yarn used as well as the qualities of knitted fabric. It pays to think ahead. Consider the seaming method you plan to use before starting to knit. For example, you may want to add an extra stitch to each edge if they will be absorbed into the seams. Many knitters hand sew their seams with invisible stitch, running stitch or backstitch. Others machine stitch their work whilst some knitters prefer to crochet seams together.

To sew up your garment, use invisible stitch – otherwise known as mattress stitch – but in any contrast colour yarn. The contrast thread means you can see exactly where the stitches are placed, but the final effect of the invisible stitch means they will not show through on the finished garment.

"I now knit to relieve work stress and create clothes that I feel proud wearing. I don't feel that empty bored feeling any more. I also don't snack at night any more and that has helped me lose a few pounds. I get a buzz from just reading a knitting magazine or feeling difficult textures in the shop. I'm also part of a knitting group who, although I don't see them often, make me feel as though there are people out there as passionate – if not more so – about it than me, makes me feel part of a community."

MEMBER OF STITCHLINKS

" *It is also true of devoted knitters that they immediately feel a connection and camaraderie when meeting a fellow knitter. There is a sense of trust that opens a door into conversation and often leads to deep, long-lasting friendships.* **"**

NANCY THOMAS & ILANA RABINOWITZ

A PASSION FOR KNITTING, 2002

There is no such a thing as too many stitch markers; they are a useful tool to the knitter. Use them to pinpoint changes in a stitch pattern, the start of rounds in circular knitting, pattern repeats, the position of motifs and all your increases and decreases. This is invaluable when picking up your knitting in odd moments as you can instantly gauge where you are in the pattern. For example, a line of stitch markers marching down a sleeve means it is easy to see when you next need to decrease and how many decreases you have already finished.

Always knit in adequate light. It is much easier to work in either bright daylight or good task lighting.

" We've started our own knitting circle on the tour bus... There's something about knitting that I love – the texture and colours and repetition. It's vaguely creative and stops me smoking. Sometimes. "

ALISON GOLDFRAPP
SINGER-SONGWRITER AND KNITTER
(1966–)

Knitting can help conquer
addiction as it occupies both
the hands and the mind. Plus
knitting can be taken anywhere –
its portability means you always
have help at hand any time a
craving strikes.

If you need to select a needle size for an unlabelled yarn, double over the yarn and thread it through the closest size hole on a needle gauge. The hole that it fits through most neatly is the best needle size for your first swatch.

"*It's a kind of trick, Dad, because it's just a long, long, fat string and it turns into a scarf.***"**

E. ANNIE PROULX
WRITER AND JOURNALIST (1935–),
THE SHIPPING NEWS, 1993

"*For me the process of knit one, purl one is the best form of therapy. I was taught to knit at infant school at the age of five, and have been knitting ever since. I recall the pleasure of making (badly) knitted scarves in lurid acrylics and on pink and yellow plastic needles. My idea of heaven!*

Fast forward to my time at Art School and my 'eureka' moment of mastering cable stitches and colour work. The knitting world was now my oyster. My future design path was set and clear."

MARTIN STOREY
DESIGNER AND KNITTER

"I find when I am sitting knitting I do not feel lazy, as I would if I just sat resting, but useful and productive. This has seriously helped me both mentally and physically. I have suffered depression over the last 3–4 years but find the boost I get from feeling "useful" really helps to lift my mood and the satisfaction of finishing a garment and the buzz of the next project really keep me going."

MEMBER OF STITCHLINKS

"*Everything I knit can be worn by someone, to protect, clothe or keep them warm. In L.M. Montgomery's Pat of Silver Bush, Pat's mother says, "How I loved to wake up in the night and feel that my husband and my children were well and safe and warm, sleeping peacefully. Life hasn't anything better to offer a woman than that, Patsy." When I knit for people, which is all my knitting, I feel like that.*"

JULIA GRUNAU
CEO OF PATTERNFISH AND KNITTER

When working the double or long-tail cast-on method, it is very irritating to near the end only to find the tail is not long enough to make the required number of stitches. So how do you know how long to make your yarn tail? As a rough guide, allow 2.5cm (1 in) per stitch to be cast on. If you don't have a tape measure to hand, however, simply wrap the yarn around the needle once for each cast-on stitch, plus a couple of times extra just to be sure. That gives you the correct length of tail.

❝ *Knitting is very conducive to thought. It is nice to knit a while, put down the needles, write a while, then take up the sock again.* **❞**

DOROTHY DAY
ACTIVIST AND KNITTER (1897–1980)

Knitting too has been around for thousands of years and, like yoga, has recently seen a boom. Why do people compare the two? There are several reasons that are usually cited. Similar to yoga, knitting forces those who practice it to slow down, to take a break from the rush of everyday tasks, to look at the parts that make the whole, and to expand themselves both mentally and physically.

RENÉE BLIXT
WRITER AND KNITTING TEACHER

If you're finding a pattern confusing
or you just can't seem to get to grips
with a certain knitting technique,
keep calm. Don't hurry, just work
through it one stitch at a time.

To prevent a ball of yarn rolling uncontrollably around the floor whilst knitting, take the hidden yarn end from the inner core of the ball – as opposed to the visible yarn end sat on its outside – and use that to cast on and knit with. You may need to scoop out the very centre of the ball and unravel it to find this end.

> **"*Knitting is the saving of life.*"**

VIRGINIA WOLF
WRITER AND KNITTER (1882–1941)

When measuring your knitting, use
a metal ruler for the most accurate
results. A conventional tailor's tape
measure can become worn and
stretched with frequent use.

Don't be afraid to try lace knitting, it is simply comprised of a combination of 'eyelets' – or open increases – and decreases. Stitches are made by taking the yarn over the needle to create a light and airy effect. The simplest lace patterns either work each increase next to the corresponding decrease in a row or the increases and decreases occur at different points along the same row. Whichever method is used, the number of stitches in each row remains constant.

"*Sometimes she knits and sits,
Sometimes she sits and knits...
And you notice a spasmodic
movement of her lips,
And you think she is going to say
something but she is only counting
the number of stitches it takes to
surround the hips;
And she furrows her beautiful brow,
which is a sign that something is
wrong somewhere and you keep on
talking, and disregard the sign,
And she casts a lethal glance, as one
who purls before swine,*

*And this goes on for weeks
At the end of which she lays her
work down and speaks,
And you think now maybe you can
have some home life but she speaks in
a tone as far off as Mercury or Saturn,
And she says thank goodness that is
finished, it is a sight and she will
never be able to wear it, but it doesn't
matter because she can hardly wait to
start on an adorable new pattern.* "

OGDEN NASH

POET (1902–1971), *MACHINERY DOESN'T ANSWER
EITHER, BUT YOU AREN'T MARRIED TO IT,* 1929

According Dr Kawashima, developer of the Brain Training Nintendo DS games, knitting activates the prefrontal cortex of the brain. This strengthens hand and eye coordination as well as keeping the brain active.

"Alice's fingers flicked up and down, making precisely the same movement about a hundred times a minute. And they seemed to move independently of the rest of Alice, of her body which was gracefully relaxed, of her eyes which occasionally met his, and of her mind too, he suspected, which might be wandering off anywhere."

RUTH RENDELL
WRITER (1930–), 'A NEEDLE FOR THE DEVIL',
THE FEVER TREE AND OTHER STORIES, 1982

Devise your own individual jacquard, Fair Isle or other stranded colourwork patterns by adapting tapestry, embroidery, cross stitch or needlepoint charts.

Many knitters swear by using lifelines in their work. A lifeline is a temporary thread that is inserted through a row of stitches, which acts like an insurance policy against the damages a mistake can cause. If you happen to drop a stitch or make some other mistake, you will only have to rip out as far back as the lifeline. The best place for a lifeline is at the beginning or end of a pattern repeat, inserted through each stitch just below the knitting needle. Some knitters use dental floss as it glides easily, but any fine thread works well.

After witnessing the "zen quality" that knitting imparted on her regular craft group, Lynn Zwerling had a light-bulb moment: she decided to spread the feel-good factor gained through knitting to a less-conventional audience. In 2009, after many knockbacks, Lynn's persistence paid off when she was invited to teach inmates at the Jessup Pre-Release Unit, Maryland, the basics of knitting. Knitting Behind Bars (knittingbehindbars. blogspot.com) is now an established organisation and Lynn's classes are so popular with prisoners there is a waiting list.

If you find knitting on straight needles leads to back or side pain, switch to a circular needle. The bulk of the weight of your knitting will then be held by the wire that sits in your lap, thereby taking the majority of the weight of the stitches off the needles and consequently your back and shoulders.

> **"***You don't knit because you are patient. You are patient because you knit.***"**

STEPHANIE PEARL-MCPHEE
WRITER AND KNITTER (1968–)
*THINGS I LEARNED FROM KNITTING…
WHETHER I WANTED TO OR NOT*, 2008

Hobbies can be great distractions. Losing yourself in the activity is the key. Try something fresh that requires you to build new skills. Both hobbies and exercise can give you a sense of accomplishment and identity that shores you up and prevents you from falling back into overthinking.

DR SUSAN NOLEN-HOEKSEMA
PROFESSOR OF PSYCHOLOGY,
YALE UNIVERSITY

When finishing a basic drop-shoulder sweater, if you are joining a straight cast-off sleeve top to the row ends of the back and front, do not match each stitch for stitch. If you skip a few row ends at regular intervals this will compensate for the different gauges of stitches and rows and avoid the little 'gather' or 'bump' that can easily appear. As a general rule of thumb, pick up approximately every one-and-a-half stitches.

After laundering, never hang a handknit up to dry as it will stretch out of shape: always dry a piece of knitting laid out flat. Likewise, never place a handknit on a coathanger: always store your knits loosely folded and flat.

" *Knitting is essentially a 'materials' process, catering to my tactile needs in the same way painting and sculpture do, but at the same time it is a complex series of systems. It's this duality that I find most appealing – satisfying tactile needs as well as the inherent need for structure, logic and order in my personal creative process. I was trained as a painter, and though I always loved painting as a material process, the lack of an underlying system always left me feeling lost. I am a 'grid' person – I've always been happy making patterns on grids, and especially drawn to geometry, pattern and texture. Which, to my delight, I found was the essential domain of knitting when I first picked up the needles. I've been constantly drawn to it as a way of exploring and solving design problems ever since.* "

JARED FLOOD
ARTIST, DESIGNER AND KNITTER

Confusion can often arise when a lace garment needs to be shaped, for example, at the armhole or increasing along a sleeve edge. Often the knitter has to use their suduko-like problem-solving skills. These tips may help: most lace patterns have a decrease for every increase made, when shaping you should regard these as pairs and do not work an increase unless you have enough stitches to work the decrease and vice versa; count the number of stitches at the end of each row, check that the increases and decreases are in the correct place above the previous pattern row; if there are not enough stitches to work both the increase and the decrease, work the few stitches at each (or either) end in the background stitch (usually stocking stitch); when only a few stitches are to be decreased, for example at an armhole or neck edge, insert a marker at the end of the first pattern repeat in from the edge; at the end of every decrease row, check that there is the correct number of stitches in both these marked sections.

"I really believe that knitting is more than a craft. Knitting has the ability to transform you."

LYNN ZWERLING
FOUNDER OF KNITTING BEHIND BARS

Remember why you knit:
for fun, for relaxation and
for making something special.

> *"There is nothing more satisfying than casting on and knitting. Passing yarn over the needle reminds me of water flowing over a stone in a stream. It is so soothing, relaxing and ultimately satisfying. You're giving time back to yourself – it's like a kind of meditation. Those who don't knit have no idea what they are missing."*

BRANDON MABLY
DESIGNER AND KNITTER

Don't get into a flap over which buttons to chose for your knitting, the choice is simple. My tried-and-tested, failsafe button preference is mother-of-pearl. The light reflected from the fragments of shell picks up the tones of the yarns, so they will always blend perfectly. I use just two colours: a natural, light hue for lighter knits and a natural, dark shade for darker knits.

"Knitting is not for the faint
of heart but hopefully patience,
anger management, goal setting and
pride will be the result of learning
this new skill."

LYNN ZWERLING,
FOUNDER OF KNITTING BEHIND BARS

"*Stitch your stress away.*"

ANONYMOUS

MAKE A SOOTHING, SWEETLY SCENTED LAVENDER BAG TO PROMOTE SLEEP.

TO MAKE A 12 X 16CM BAG, you need 50g of 4-ply yarn, pair of 2.00mm needles, length of fine ribbon, some thin muslin and lavender seedheads.

Using 2.00mm needles, cast on 83 sts. Work 12cm in stocking stitch, ending with a purl row.
Eyelet row: k5, * yarn forward, k2tog, k8, rep from * to last 6 sts, k to end.
Work a further 3cm in stocking stitch, ending with a purl row.
Picot edge: cast off 3 sts, * slip stitch on

right-hand needle back on to left-hand needle, cast on 2 sts, cast off 5 sts, rep from * to end of row. Cast off last stitch.

TO MAKE UP: fold knitting in half widthways with right sides together and picot edge at the top. Seam along side and bottom edges. Thread fine ribbon through all eyelets. Cut a rectangle of muslin 12cm wide by 26cm deep. Fold in half lengthwise and sew the two side seams, leaving the top edge open. Fill bag with lavender seedheads. Turn top edge over and sew. Insert lavender sachet into knitted bag, pull up the ribbon and tie in a decorative bow at the front.

"When I sit down to knit, especially during lunch hours, I have to do an internal switching of gears in order to focus solely on knitting. It is refreshing to concentrate totally on just one thing, especially something that is creative. Knowing that this total focus leads to productivity helps me bring that level of concentration to other things."

MEMBER OF STITCHLINKS

Research at Harvard Medical School Mind Body Institute has found that when an individual is knitting their heart rate can drop up to 11 beats per minute along with a drop in blood pressure.

"Now your old dame gives this advice to the rising generation: that whilst children are young they learn to knit, whatever may be their station."

RACHEL JANE CATLOW

FROM A DAME TO HER SCHOLARS

When making up a garment, follow this order of assembly. For a sweater knitted flat in pieces, join the shoulder seams first. Next, attach the sleeves. Finally, sew the side and underarm seams. Use long, straight pins to join the pieces together before seaming. After sewing, neaten the seams by lightly steaming them with an iron.

"*Knitting, I believe, saved my life. But is also introduced me to a new world of yarn and colours and textures and of people. Sitting in various knitting circles, I slowly learned that knitting had rescued other women too. Bad marriages, illness, addiction — knitting gave comfort and even hope through life's trials.*"

ANN HOOD
WRITER AND KNITTER (1956–)

"I found that knitting helped calm my thoughts. While I was knitting and putting stitches in order, it was easier to put my own mind in order."

MEMBER OF STITCHLINKS

Never weave in a yarn end vertically up the side of your knitting as this makes for a lumpy and distorted edge.

Always measure your knitting on
a clean, flat surface, rather than on
your lap, the side of your armchair
or the carpet. It is acceptable to
measure your work upright, hanging
from the needle, when you are
making something that is likely to
'drop' or stretch vertically,
such as a heavy yarn like cotton or
viscose. However, a well-designed
pattern should account for this.

> *"I was a foolhardy lover who has always been prepared to throw his loyalty and devotion at the feet of Mistress Knitting."*

JAMES NORBURY
DESIGNER, TELEVISION PERSONALITY
AND KNITTER (1904–1972)

If your knitting is getting the better of you, sometimes the simple solution is to ask another knitter for a little help. If you don't have a fellow knitter in your circle of friends, family or neighbours, log on to an online knitting forum. If the answer to your dilemma isn't already out there, another knitter is bound to be willing to share their expertise and experience.

A study conducted by the Mayo Clinic, Minnesota, found that activities such as knitting during later years are good for your brain. "Quilting and knitting, these types of intellectual activities, might be somewhat neuroprotective," says Dr Yonas Geda. The study showed a 30–50% decrease in developing memory loss for those engaged in activities like knitting, which may be beneficial for delaying the onset of dementia.

"I knit because it's calming, or challenging; it's like an endlessly changing puzzle, mood-specific sudoku. I knit because I can make the useful beautiful; or the sensual practical — and vice versa. I knit because you can build the embellishment into the piece itself as you go, and eschew needles frippery — unless you want it. I knit to connect myself to history."

JULIA GRUNAU
CEO OF PATTERNFISH AND KNITTER

When you are making up a project,
use glass-headed pins so that when
you come to remove them, they
are more readily visible. Once you
have finished sewing up, always
doublecheck your knitting for any
stray pins. I once forgot to do this –
to a friend's peril!

Much can be learnt from the traditional techniques used to make Guernsey sweaters. The knotted cast on is one such technique, which gives a distinctive, decorative and robust edge. Leaving a yarn end that is approximately four times the length of the edge to be cast on, make a slip knot on one needle. Cast on one stitch by the single or thumb cast-on method, lift the slip knot over this cast-on stitch. Cast on a further two stitches and take the first of these over the second. Repeat this last step for each cast-on stitch.

> **"***You knit with great skill, madame.***"**
> "*I am accustomed to it.*"
> "*A pretty pattern too!*"
> "*You think so?*" *said madame, looking at him with a smile.*
> "*Decidedly. May one ask what it is for?*"
> "*Pastime,*" *said madame, looking at him with a smile, while her fingers moved nimbly.***"**

CHARLES DICKENS
WRITER (1812–1870),
A TALE OF TWO CITIES, 1859

When you get home from a long day at work, instead of reaching for a tub of ice cream or a glass of wine, pick up your knitting. You'll enjoy the relaxing benefits of this calming craft and save yourself the calories of ice cream or the alcohol units of wine.

If a pattern calls for using the yarn
double, this simply means knitting
with two strands instead of just one.
Rather than using two separate balls
of yarn, take one yarn end from the
outside of a ball and then find the
other yarn end at the core of the same
ball – this way you are knitting from
both ends of a single ball of yarn.

When shaping within colour knitting, use the lifted strand increase where a stitch is made by lifting the horizontal strand that lies between two stitches. Make sure the lifted strand lies on the left-hand needle in the same direction as all the other stitches, then simply knit into the back of it to create an extra stitch.

If your stitches fall off the needle, don't panic. Firstly, take a deep breath. Secondly, think about the way the stitches are supposed to sit on the needle. Look at the loop and notice that it has a 'right leg' and a 'left leg'. Slip the stitches back on to the needle, one at a time, in the same order they were in and so that no stitches are missed or twisted. If, when you go to knit it, a stitch feels tight, fix it by either taking the stitch off the needle, untwisting it and sliding it back onto the needle or by knitting into the back of the stitch.

"*I'm both a product and a process knitter. Product as I love to wear a beautifully crafted knits and process as making the stitches has such a calming effect. We all need stillness in our lives and when I'm running on empty and feeling stressed, I always turn to either my guitar or my knitting. It's a haven for me and it's certainly saved my life more than a couple of times.*"

JEAN MOSS
DESIGNER AND KNITTER

In the euphoria of finishing a project, it is easy to race through the making up of a garment. However, blocking makes a huge difference. When properly blocked, the tension of a piece of knitting evens out, the yarn blooms and the fabric plumps up. Sometimes you need only to dunk the knitting, squeeze out any excess water, then pin it into the right size and shape for drying. Other times you need to steam the knitting, stretch it carefully to size, then allow to dry. Occasionally you must pin out the piece, spritz with water and leave to dry.

If using a fluffy yarn, such as mohair
or angora, when you are taking a
break from your knitting, place the
ball in a polythene bag and store it
in the refrigerator. When kept cool,
fluffy yarn is easier to work with.

"*Nowhere is design more important. Discard design and a knitted garment can quickly become dowdy. Overdesign it and it becomes a mess. We are at our best working within such strict confines.*"

SIR HARDY AMIES
DESIGNER AND DRESSMAKER (–2003)

Sometimes, keeping it simple works
best: simple stitch with a beautiful
yarn in your favourite colour.

When joining in a new colour at the beginning of a row, the first stitch can become loose. To ensure a firm start, insert the needle into the first stitch and take both the old and the new yarn round the needle and through the stitch. Then, using only the new yarn but doubled, knit the next two stitches. Continue with just a single strand of the new yarn to the end of the row. On the return row treat the double yarn as single stitches and knit the last two stitches together.

When knitting a sweater, it doesn't always have to have a rib edge or welt. Experiment with some more unexpected stitches to create a border; a lacy edge to an aran sweater can look very pretty.

Instead of knitting a cardigan back and fronts separately, work them all together as one piece. Count up the stitches needed for each individual piece, including the stitches required for the button bands, add them together and cast on this number. You will most likely need to work on circular needles for this volume of stitches. Continue on these stitches until you reach the armhole shaping, then divide the stitches. This cuts down on sewing up and gives a seamless and fluid finish.

"*As I get older,
I just prefer to knit.***"**

TRACEY ULLMAN
ACTOR, COMEDIAN, WRITER
AND KNITTER (1959–)

"The fact that I could follow a pattern and be able to concentrate for long periods has done wonders for my self esteem as has admiring the finished article."

MEMBER OF STITCHLINKS

When pressing a finished knitting project, always check the ball band before applying any hot steam. Natural fibres can take heat, however, man-made fibres need a cool, dry press otherwise they will collapse. Take care not to overpress a finished piece of knitting. A correctly pressed knit should not look like it has been ironed flat, instead it should be smooth and even. When correctly blocked or pressed, your yarn should bloom.

Most patterns give the tension over 10cm (4 inches) square, but working a 15cm (6 inches) square works best. Not only does a slightly larger square give a truer measurement, the swatch can be put to use afterwards.

Experiment with colour. Take a small repeating pattern, such as a little Fair Isle motif, and try changing the background colour. Navy and black are always great bases and work well to coordinate with prints in your existing wardrobe. Then place the exact same colour Fair Isle motif on an ecru background to give a totally fresh approach.

"*It is the wealth of different yarns and fibres available that makes knitting an exciting creative medium. I adore pattern and colour foremost, and that is what inspires my designing. I design a garment shape to compliment the fabric. Knitting is wonderful as it can create fabrics that drape, add dimension through cabling and partial knitting and also fit the body beautifully. It can be a work of art. I especially love hand knitting as you create something unique – after all no two hand knitters knit the same. Any garment made by hand is alive with the creator's personality, an individualism which simply is not achievable through machine knitting.* **"**

MARIE WALLIN
HEAD DESIGNER AT ROWAN YARNS

Knitting is a bit like meditation.
Instead of maybe using a sound you
are actually using a physical repetition.
By repeating the same action over and
over again it becomes almost like a
trance-like state, which creates general
relaxation and helps to reduce stress.

PAUL HANDFORTH
APS LIFE COACHING

Should you find that your knitting is
uneven, it may be that you are faster
and looser on the knit rows and tighter
and slower on the purl rows. To fix
an uneven surface, use different size
needles: try a smaller needle for the
knit rows and a size larger needle for
the purl rows.

Using a crochet hook instead of a knitting needle makes casting off faster, easier and neater, plus it doesn't stretch the stitches. You can use a crochet hook on any stitch pattern, including rib. Holding the working yarn in your left hand, slip the first stitch on to the crochet hook. Insert the hook into the second stitch, catch the yarn and pull it through both stitches. Repeat until there is just one stitch on the hook, break off the yarn then pull it through this last stitch.

If you are struggling to knit
socks on a set of double-pointed
needles, try knitting them on two
circular needles instead.

" *Useful and ornamental needlework, knitting, and netting are capable of being made, not only sources of personal gratification, but of high moral benefit, and the means of developing in surpassing loveliness and grace, some of the highest and noblest feelings of the soul.* **"**

ANONYMOUS

THE LADIES' WORK-TABLE BOOK, 1845

Slipping the first stitch and knitting the last stitch of every row will give a really neat edge to your knitting.

Knitting is promoted by Stitchlinks as a tool that can teach life skills such as planning and goal setting.

If you make a mistake and need to rip out a few rows, mark the erroneous stitch with a safety pin. Alternatively, if you are working in a fine yarn, you may prefer to thread a 'safety line' of yarn through the stitches of the preceding good row of knitting. Slide all the stitches from the needle then steadily undo each row, winding in the yarn. As you near the marked mistake, slow down and place each unravelled stitch back on to the needle one by one; you don't want to unravel any more stitches than is strictly necessary.

When knitting a sweater, if you know that either a stitch or a yarn is going to create a heavy fabric, work one or two centimetres less in the length, one centimetre less before the armhole shaping and one centimetre less after the armhole shaping. This adjustment will allow for the sweater 'dropping' with wear.

Always read the pattern through
carefully before you start knitting.
This sounds obvious, but it does save
a lot of ripping out.

"I sometimes have a lot of stress in my life, and I don't always handle it very well. I am impatient and quick to anger, and though I try to manage this with other strategies… knitting is the only thing that calms me completely. Everything else is a temporary remedy until I can knit. I often have knitting with me, something small to work on while waiting in lines, or to take with me on my lunch hour."

MEMBER OF STITCHLINKS

" *Everybody tells me that they would love to knit, but they don't have time. I look at people's lives and I can see opportunity and time for knitting all over the place. The time spent riding the bus each day? That's a pair of socks over a month. Waiting in line? Mittens. Watching TV? Buckets of wasted time that could be an exquisite lace shawl.* "

STEPHANIE PEARL-MCPHEE
WRITER AND KNITTER (1968–),
*AT KNIT'S END: MEDITATIONS FOR
WOMEN WHO KNIT TOO MUCH,* 2005

All you need in order to knit is two sticks and some continuous thread. Experiment with string, ribbon, raffia, wire and leather. Alternatively, rip strips of cotton fabric – gingham and ticking are my favourites – and join them with knots, or cut spirals from plastic bags, soft leather or suede. If you can make a continuous thread of it, you can knit it!

Avoid joining in a yarn in the middle
of a row. If you have enough yarn
to stretch three times across the rest
of the row, you will have enough to
finish knitting it.

" *I like making a piece of string into something I can wear.* "

ANONYMOUS

A tight cast-on will not make a firmer edge, in fact the opposite is true. An edge that pulls will soon snap with strain. To avoid this try the following: pull the yarn a little looser; cast on with a larger size needle; cast on a few more stitches and then decrease evenly across the first row. On the other hand a loose cast-on will ruckle and not look good.

To avoid this try the following: pull yarn a little tighter; cast on with a smaller size needle; cast on fewer stitches and then increase evenly across the first row.

It is not always possible to obtain the yarn specified in a pattern as yarn companies delete lines seasonally, or you may just wish to substitute a different, preferred brand or use up yarn from your stash. This is where a correct tension is vital. But just as important is the yarn's yardage. Yardage varies according to the fibre: for example, cotton is heavier than wool, so you get less yardage for the same weight. It is important to buy the correct yardage to complete a project, rather than rely on the number of balls or weight of yarn.

A 'yarnover' is the most common increase in lace patterns. This increase is made by simply wrapping the yarn once around the right-hand needle, but without working any stitches with the left-hand needle.

"*Knitting appeals to me because it is so portable and low in tools. I can grab two needles or, better yet, one circular needle and a bag of scrap ends of lots of colours, jump on a train, a plane or in a car and knit up a set of patterns in luscious combinations of colour.*

The trip goes by without stress and I arrive home with an idea for a garment or throw to be done on a larger scale... I can conceive best on the needles, ideas flowing without too much cogitation. So knitting becomes my most immediate medium to organise my colour ideas."

KAFFE FASSETT
ARTIST, DESIGNER AND KNITTER (1937–)

Instead of spending money on expensive stitch markers, use either cheap coloured ponytail hairbands from a pharmacist or elastic bands from a stationery supplier. They both come in large packs in a variety of shades so you can colour-code your markers. Once you no longer need the marker, simply snip off the band and remove it without any harm to the knitting. And unlike many purpose-made markers, elastic bands do not distort the stitches.

One of my favourite stitches is garter stitch – in which every row is a knit row – but it can be heavy. If I want a similar appearance to garter stitch but a less weighty effect, I often substitute reverse stocking stitch.

"Knitting benefits an individual's emotional and physical health. Knitting can reduce stress in an individual who is trying to manage the severity of their chronic illness. It can also help reduce stress in individuals who lead very hectic lifestyles."

GARY SCHOLAR
HEALTH AND WELLNESS CONSULTANT,
AMERICAN HOSPITAL ASSOCIATION.

Knit both the sleeves of a sweater on
the same needle and at the same time,
but using a separate ball of yarn for
each. Not only does this seem to save
time, all increases and decreases on
both sleeves will be an exact match.

Keep calm. It's only yarn. And yarn can be reknitted. So you can always rip out a few stitches or rows, track back to where you were in the pattern and start knitting again.

" *'Life is a stocking,'*
grandma says,
And yours has just begun,
But I am knitting
the toe of mine,
And my work is almost done. **"**

NINETEENTH-CENTURY RHYME

Members of Stitchlinks have
benefitted from the improved self-
confidence, sense of achievement
and feelings of success that
knitting offers.

Think about making your tension
swatches into a project, such as
a patchwork cushion, a baby's
stroller blanket, lavender-scented
sachets or even frame them as a
small picture. After all, you have
created your own little masterpiece
and it ought to be shown off.

"*From now on, I'm only going to make things that are E-A-S-Y. If it has more than fifty rows, it's out. So forget what I said about scarves last week – now, it's only Barbie scarves. And only in garter stitch. I am so done with purling.*"

KATE JACOBS

WRITER AND KNITTER, *THE FRIDAY NIGHT KNITTING CLUB*, 2007

When you are starting a sweater on
circular needles, the first rib row can
easily become twisted. To prevent
this from happening, when knitting
the initial stitch of the first rib row
that joins the two end, knit into the
back of the stitch.

A circular needle, also known as a wire, has two pointed ends joined by a length of flexible nylon of varying lengths. A circular needle makes the working of a large number of stitches easier to cope with. Not only are circular needles great for working socks, throws and seamless sweaters or cardigans, they are useful when knitting a Fair Isle. Knitted in the round, you are always working the right-side knit row thereby making colourwork that little bit easier.

Cast on your stitches with
a size larger needle than the
pattern states to ensure that
first row is not too tight.

"The yarn forms the stitches, the knitting forges the friendships, the craft links the generations."

KAREN ALFKE
DESIGNER AND KNITTER

"Knitting has been my lifesaver, I think because I can wear stuff that I have made. It fills my world with colour and pleasure and sound. My children and husband think my creations are wonderful and many friends and family have accessories that I have designed and created. I don't feel afraid anymore about feeling down or unwell I know that my knitting will keep me connected with those that love me and that I love back in return."

MEMBER OF STITCHLINKS

To avoid having to weave in all those
stray yarn ends once you've finished
knitting, knit them in as you work.
Using the same stranding technique
for colour work, knit the yarn in to the
back of the row across a few stitches.

> *" If the knitter is weary,*
> *the baby will have*
> *no new bonnet. "*

IRISH PROVERB

If you suffer from arthritis or joint pain, do not knit for overly long periods. But do not stop knitting altogether. Many knitters find that brief bouts of knitting actually improve flexibility and mobility in the joints. It is important, however, to take regular breaks to stretch your fingers.

Work any increases and decreases one, two, three or even more stitches inside the edge of your knitting. This gives a beautiful 'fully fashioned' effect to a garment as well as a lovely design detail. It also makes sewing up so much easier too.

"*There is no right way to knit; there is no wrong way to knit. So if anybody kindly tells you that what you are doing is 'wrong,' don't take umbrage; they mean well. Smile submissively, and listen, keeping your disagreement on an entirely mental level.*

They may be right, in this particular case, and even if not, they may drop off pieces of information which will come in very handy if you file them away carefully in your brain for future reference. **"**

ELIZABETH ZIMMERMANN
WRITER AND KNITTER (1910–1999),
KNITTING WITHOUT TEARS, 1971

Blocking – or pinning out – and pressing makes an enormous difference to the finish of a handknit project. To block a piece of knitting, soak it in lukewarm water, roll it in a towel to remove most of the moisture – but do not wring it out – and then pin it to a blocking board, ironing board or other flat surface, such as a towel laid over a carpet, and wait for it to dry. This may take 2–3 days, depending on the yarn.

Don't skip any stitches along the shaped edges of a neckline when picking up for a neckband; work into every decrease and row end.

When giving a hand-knitted gift, always include a ball band from the yarn in the parcel. By doing so the recipient will know the best way to launder and care for the knit.

" Given good yarn, good workmanship, and good care, a knitted shawl can outlive its knitter, providing warmth and pleasure to several generations of family and friends. "

MARTHA WATERMAN

WRITER AND KNITTER, *TRADITIONAL KNITTED LACE SHAWLS*, 1993

Stitch markers are the key
to trouble-free lace knitting.
Consistently count the stitches on
your needle within each section of
the pattern whenever you reach a
stitch marker.

Schools in the US, from Oregon
to New Jersey, are incorporating
knitting into their curriculum, not
only for the health benefits, but to
help build creativity and improve
mathematical skills.

KEEP CALM AND CAST ON

" The information is now in your hands for you to enjoy in the way that suits you best. Learn it all, or learn a little — the choice is yours. Have fun."

MONTSE STANLEY
DESIGNER, WRITER AND KNITTER
(1942–1999), *KNITTER'S HANDBOOK*, 1986

To save on sewing up and to create a professional 'selvedge edge', knit in vertical button and buttonhole bands as you work. Simply add the number of stitches needed for each band to the stitches cast on for the fronts and work them at the same time, knitting or purling as stated in the pattern.

Cover a padded ironing board with a piece of gingham or other check fabric. The grid formed by the lines of the fabric design provide a helpful guide when pinning out – simply line up the rows and stitches of the knitting to the lines of the fabric ironing board cover.

The nylon wire joining the two points of a circular needle should be straightened before use. To do this, briefly immerse the wire in a bowl of hot water, remove and then pull to straighten.

"Knitting has given me hope and a true belief in me, even though others have always believed me to be capable of doing anything I wanted, I have always doubted that, and the "stitching" has some how encouraged me otherwise."

MEMBER OF STITCHLINKS

In some of the more exquisite lace patterns the increases and decreases are made on different rows so keeping track of the number of stitches can be more 'testing'. Persevere as it is well worth the result. Lace knitting can be used in many different ways, as an all-over pattern, as a horizontal or vertical pattern or as single or random motifs.

"*I've been knitting since my mum taught me at the age of six and I've never stopped. I knit for sheer enjoyment and relaxation, I knit plain things to give myself time to think or watch TV. If I have worries, I knit more complex patterns, then I need to empty my mind to concentrate on getting every stitch right. The satisfaction that I have knitted every little stitch to make something still fills me with awe. For me, giving a knitted gift is precious as each stitch has been an action I have taken to make something lovely for someone. I hope my knitting will bring a little joy. Even now, running my little shop, I love to help my customers choose their projects and yarns, I feel excited for them to be taking their yarn home and getting started.*"

CAROLINE WILBOR
PROPRIETOR OF THE WOOL BAR
AND KNITTER

" Any number of times I have proven one of my favorite sayings: a repeated mistake may become a new design. "

MEG SWANSEN
WRITER AND KNITTER

If you are inserting a lace panel into a stocking stitch pattern, check that the tension is the same. Many lace patterns have a looser stitch tension than stocking stitch and you must allow for this.

When working a lace pattern check
that the number of stitches is correct
at the end of each row. If there are
too few, you will probably find that
a 'yarn forward' has been missed.
Check back along the row to see
where the mistake has been made.

> **"***Women like to sit
> down with trouble –
> as if it were knitting.***"**

ELLEN GLASGOW
WRITER AND SUFFRAGETTE (1873–1945)

When picking up a given number of stitches along an edge – to make, for example, a neckband or a buttonhole band – fold the edge in half and mark the halfway point, then fold each in half again and mark the quarter points. Divide the number of stitches to be picked up by the number of sections – four – and make sure you pick up the correct amount of stitches evenly from each quarter.

Instead of knitting complicated buttonholes and then sewing on buttons, cheat! Use snap fasteners instead. Not only does this look more contemporary and sporty, it is also so much simpler to do. If you want the extra detail that a button gives, you can always add one on top of the snap fastener.

Knitting socially fosters a
feeling of belonging, enjoyment
in a shared activity and
mutual friendship.

"*I like hanging around people who knit. They are usually in a good mood.***"**

MARK FRAUENFELDER
JOURNALIST, BLOGGER
AND ILLUSTRATOR

Once you have completed the knitting stage of a project, it is time to move on to finishing. Finishing comprises of weaving in any loose yarn ends that hang off your work, blocking your knitting to the correct measurements, then putting the pieces together by sewing seams. Although most knitters prefer knitting, mastering the finishing techniques will ensure you are happy with your completed projects.

Always chose the correct length of circular needle according to the number of stitches being knitted. It is preferable to have a lot of stitches on a shorter wire as you can always bunch the stitches together. Too few stitches on a circular needle and they will be stretched and will not cover the circumference of the needle.

> **"** *Of all the husbands*
> *of the earth,*
> *The sailor has the finest berth,*
> *For in 'is cabin he can sit,*
> *And sail and sail*
> *and let 'er knit.* **"**

WALLACE IRWIN
POET (1875–1959),
NAUTICAL LAYS OF A LANDSMAN, 1904

When working a favourite aran sweater pattern, ring the changes by substituting a stitch panel with a different textured stitch pattern that knits to the same tension or a cable that is worked over the same number of stitches.

If your circle joins are untidy when circular knitting, use one of the following remedies: pull the yarn firmly at the join; cast on an extra stitch and decrease; cast on an extra stitch and decrease over the first and second cast-on stitches.

"I come from a long line of knitters, crocheters, dressmakers and textile enthusiasts, so it is no wonder that I was born with the urge to make beautiful fabric. Art school honed my colour sense and repeating patterns soothed my mind. Hand knitting combines colour, texture, pattern and graphic design, which, when shaken and stirred, gives me a wearable canvas for my creativity."

SASHA KAGAN
DESIGNER AND KNITTER

" *Whenever I would take up the needles I would feel myself connected not only to my own mother, grandmother, and great-grandmother, but also to the women who lived centuries before me, the women who had developed the craft, the women who had known, as I did, the incredible satisfaction and sense of serenity that could come from the steady, rhythmic click-click-click of one's knitting needles. These women had experienced the meditative and peaceful quality* *that overcomes one's mind while knitting; they understood the way that one's thoughts get worked right into one's knitting, discovering, as I did, that whatever I was thinking about when I last worked on a piece would immediately spring back into my mind when I picked up the work again later on, as though knitting were a sort of mental tape recorder.*"

DEBBIE STOLLER
WRITER, JOURNALIST AND KNITTER,
STITCH 'N BITCH: THE KNITTER'S HANDBOOK, 2003

The simplest way to pick up stitches along a vertical edge is to hold the knitting with the right side facing you, insert the needle one stitch in from the side edge, wrap the yarn around the tip of the needle knitwise, then pull a loop of yarn through to make a stitch. Repeat until you have picked up sufficient stitches. When you continue to knit on these stitches, remember the pick-up row is a wrong side row.

> *"If you don't knit, bring a book."*

DOROTHY PARKER
THEATRE CRITIC, WRITER, SATIRIST AND
KNITTER (1893–1993), REVIEW OF A
MUSICAL COMEDY, *VANITY FAIR*, 1918

"Knitting helps me maintain the mobility in my hands. It is painful and difficult to get moving in the morning, and without the motivation of knitting for my grandchildren, I think my fingers would have seized up long ago."

MEMBER OF STITCHLINKS

When casting on, casting off, joining in new yarn or cutting a yarn end, always leave at least a 15cm (6 in) tail. This makes managing yarn ends easier as you need at least that length to weave in a tail properly. If the yarn ends you leave are too short, they can work loose and your knitting may unravel.

If you are knitting with a bulky, super-
bulky or highly textured novelty yarn,
you may find that using the same
yarn for seaming adds too much bulk.
When making up, use a smooth yarn
for seaming that matches in colour and
requires similar aftercare.

" I find that knitting offers me so much – from the simple project as relaxation to the sheer joy of textured and lace patterns, which seem to magically appear on the needles. I find there is a knitting project to match just about every mood and moment. "

SARAH HATTON
DESIGNER AND KNITTER

"My knitting was – and is – always with me. Keeping me company. Protecting me in the vulnerable times and giving people an easy way of communicating with me. As an adult I unfortunately have been diagnosed with a stress-related depression and use my knitting as a place, a hobby all mine, and just for me. A place I can be meditative and just feel the structure of the yarn and the almost hypnotic click-clack of the needles. It helps me heal."

MEMBER OF STITCHLINKS

While some knitters love making up and finishing off their work, and enjoy making their knitting look as professional as possible, others hate it. If you fall into the latter camp, there is no shame in hiring someone to do it for you while you carry on with your more pleasurable knitting.

A picot cast-on gives a very pretty edge to an otherwise classic garment. The picots can be made on every stitch so the edge will 'flare' or they can be spaced with as many chain cast-off stitches between as needed to make the edge 'flat.' Insert the right-hand needle into the first stitch on the left-hand needle and knit one stitch, but do not slip it off the needle, instead make a second new stitch as before. Cast off four stitches, then slip the remaining stitch back onto the left-hand needle. Repeat across the row, making two stitches and casting off four each time.

"*It takes balls to knit.*"

STEVE MALCOLM
BLOGGER

"*I see myself as a designer first, then a knitwear designer, but the beauty of designing hand knits is you get to create the fabric as well. Assessing how the yarn behaves, determining where the pattern should start and finish, creating almost architectural 'landscapes' of texture in an aran, all this makes the design process a fascinating one.*"

DEBBIE BLiSS
DESIGNER AND KNITTER

If you do find your yarn ends are too short to be woven in easily, turn a tapestry needle upside down and use the 'eye' to take the yarn end through the stitches. Alternatively, use a crochet hook to catch the yarn and pull the end through the backs of as many stitches as possible.

> *" In through the front door,*
> *Once around the back,*
> *Peek through the window,*
> *And off jumps Jack. "*

CHILDREN'S NURSERY RHYME
FOR REMEMBERING THE KNIT STITCH

> *"Down through the bunny hole,*
> *Around the big tree,*
> *Up pops the bunny*
> *And off goes she."*

CHILDREN'S NURSERY RHYME
FOR REMEMBERING THE PURL STITCH

" *She turned again to Mrs. Ansley, but the latter had reached a delicate point in her knitting. "One, two, three — slip two; yes, they must have been," she assented, without looking up. Mrs. Slade's eyes rested on her with a deepened attention. "She can knit — in the face of this! How like her…"* **"**

EDITH WHARTON
WRITER (1862–1937), *ROMAN FEVER*, 1934

Knitting can facilitate relaxation
and mindful meditation.

When picking up stitches from a piece worked in a specific stitch pattern, space the stitches as necessary to fit in with the pattern.

"*Knitting is a boon for those of us who are easily bored. I take my knitting everywhere to take the edge off of moments that would otherwise drive me stark raving mad.*"

STEPHANIE PEARL-MCPHEE
WRITER AND KNITTER (1968–),
AT KNIT'S END: MEDITATIONS FOR WOMEN WHO KNIT TOO MUCH, 2005

"*Knitters who have been at it a while experience a trancelike state that provides the same benefits as other forms of meditation. Unlike other forms of meditation, though, when all is said and done, knitting produces beautiful, handcrafted, wearable works of art.*

Each garment reflects its unique moment in time and is as singular in its construction as the person who knit it — an image of its creator's spirit. "

BERNADETTE MURPHY
WRITER AND KNITTER,
ZEN AND THE ART OF KNITTING, 2002

" Really, all you need to become a good knitter are wool, needles, hands, and slightly below-average intelligence. Of course, superior intelligence, such as yours and mine, is an advantage. "

ELIZABETH ZIMMERMANN
WRITER AND KNITTER (1910–1999),
KNITTING WITHOUT TEARS, 1971

Every stitch is part of something bigger. Each added stitch brings you closer to a finished product. Almost nothing can be created without parts smaller than itself. It's hard not to think of the item's recipient while knitting, and knitters say that each stitch is like saying a prayer for, or meditating on, the recipient. How freeing it is to stop thinking about problems and hand yourself over to a couple of hours of peace and quiet.

RENÉE BLIXT
WRITER AND KNITTING TEACHER

Mark your knitting with a
contrasting finer or texture yarn
every 20 rows. This makes easy work
of counting rows on dark yarn at
night or in poor light.

*" People knit for many reasons —
creative expression, gifts of love,
to prove they can. I knit for all of
these reasons and more: knitting
is my therapy. Knitting is my
meditation. The quiet geometry
of stitches, the dance of color, and
the soft yielding yarn displace the
thoughts that I cannot release."*

SUZYN JACKSON
WRITER, JEWELLERY DESIGNER
AND KNITTER

Dr Herbert Bendon, Director of the Institute for Mind, Body Medicine at Massachusetts General Hospital and Associate Professor of Medicine at Harvard Medical School, found in a study that knitting is an effective method of creating a "relaxation response" in the body, which can lower blood pressure, heart rate and help prevent illness.

> **"** *There!" said Mother irritably, "you've made me lose count. I do wish you wouldn't argue with me when I'm knitting.* **"**

GERALD DURRELL
WRITER (1925–1995), *MY FAMILY AND OTHER ANIMALS*, 1956

For more information on Stitchlinks, visit www.stitchlinks.com
For more information on Knitting Behind Bars, visit knittingbehindbars.blogspot.com

Editorial Director Jane O'Shea
Creative Director Helen Lewis
Series Editor Lisa Pendreigh
Designer Claire Peters
Production Director Vincent Smith
Production Controller Aysun Hughes

First published in 2011 by
Quadrille Publishing Limited
Alhambra House, 27–31 Charing Cross Road, London WC2H 0LS
www.quadrille.co.uk

Reprinted in 2012
10 9 8 7 6 5 4 3 2

Text © 2011 Erika Knight
Design and layout © 2011 Quadrille Publishing Limited

Cataloguing in Publication Data: a catalogue record for this book is available from
the British Library.

ISBN 978 184949 095 5

Printed in China